One of the two initial prototypes put on the road in October 1957. The A35 grille was intended to confuse casual observers. The engine was the 948 cc Minor/A35 A-series unit.

THE MINI

Jon Pressnell

Shire Publications Ltd

CONTENTS

Issigonis before the Mini 3
Design and development 6
The range expands 11
Foreign variants, British experimentation, and model development 17
The Mini in competition 23
Replacing the Mini 26
The Mini's twilight years 29
Further reading 32
Places to visit and clubs 32

Published in 2012 by Shire Publications Ltd, Midland House, West Way, Botley Oxford OX2 0PH, UK. Website: www.shirebooks.co.uk

Copyright © 1994 by Jon Pressnell. First edition 1994; reprinted 1997, 2001, 2004, 2010, 2011 and 2012. Shire Library 299.

ISBN-13: 978 0 74780 235 8.

Printed in China through Worldprint Ltd.

British Library Cataloguing in Publication Data: Pressnell, Jon. Mini. – (Shire Library: No. 299). I. Title. II. Series. 629.222. ISBN 0-7478-0235-1.

Cover: *Illustration from an early sales brochure for the Austin Seven version of the BMC Mini. This brochure was intended for the US market, hence the steering wheel on the left.*

ACKNOWLEDGEMENTS

The author is very grateful to the following for their invaluable assistance: Anders Clausager and Karam Ram at the British Motor Industry Heritage Trust; Kevin Jones, John Chasemore and Rod Barnes at Rover Cars; Alex Moulton, John Sheppard, Chris Kingham, Charles Griffin, Fred Coultas and Jack Daniels, for their reminiscences of working with Sir Alec Issigonis. The photographs in this Album are drawn from four sources: Rover Group, pages 1, 6, 18 (upper and lower centre, bottom), 19 (top), 30 (bottom), 31; the British Motor Industry Heritage Trust, pages 5, 7, 9, 13 (centre, bottom), 14 (lower centre), 26; the Haymarket Magazines motoring photograph library, pages 3, 4, 13 (top), 16 (centre), 18 (top), 19 (bottom), 20 (bottom), 21 (top), 22 (centre, bottom), 24, 25 (top); and the author's own collection, all remaining photographs.

A typical Issigonis sketch, depicting the Mini. It is interesting in that it shows the car with its revised east-west engine layout (ignition to the front), but with the rear trailing arms mounted directly on the body rather than attached to a subframe.

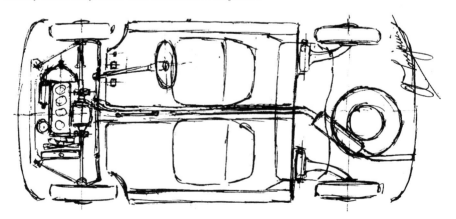

The Lightweight Special built by Alec Issigonis and his friend George Dowson between 1933 and 1938. It has a stressed-skin construction, using aluminum-covered plywood; the seat pan, engine and axle casing contribute to structural rigidity. The suspension is by rubber discs at the front and rubber loops at the rear.

ISSIGONIS BEFORE THE MINI

The Mini was largely the creation of one man, in a way which would be impossible to imagine in today's motor industry. That man was Alec Issigonis, one of the greatest and most inspired motor engineers of the twentieth century.

Born in 1906, Issigonis joined Morris Motors in 1936. After a period working on front suspension systems and – during the Second World War – on various military projects, he became responsible for the design of what became the Morris Minor.

Before that, in the period 1933-8 Issigonis and his friend George Dowson built a racing special based on the Austin Seven. Although home-constructed, without the use of power tools, the so-called Lightweight Special was more advanced than most Grand Prix cars of the day. In particular, it had a brilliantly conceived monocoque form of construction in which many elements were given a structural function with which they would not nor-mally have been entrusted; it also had rubber springing, with rubber discs at the front and rubber loops in tension at the rear. The lessons that would lead to the Mini were in the process of being learnt.

The Morris Minor was essentially an imaginative interpretation of conventional engineering practices. It was, however, a car of exceptional subtlety in its details, and it displayed characteristics which were to reappear in the Mini. Notable among these were a wheel-at-each-corner stance, smaller wheels than normal, excellent space utilisation, and first-rate roadhold-ing and handling.

The next step was to aim for front-wheel drive, as used on the Citroën *Traction Avant* which Issigonis so admired. In 1952, therefore, a front-wheel-drive trans-verse-engined Minor was created. It proved successful, but before it was com-pleted Issigonis had left for Alvis, with a brief to design an all-new sports saloon. He was at Alvis until 1955, when this

ambitious project was unfortunately abandoned, and he then returned to the British Motor Corporation, which had been formed in 1952 by a merger between Morris's parent company, the Nuffield Organisation, and the Austin Motor Company.

The Alvis saloon played an important part in the development of the Mini – in two ways. Firstly, it cemented Issigonis's personal and professional friendship with suspension engineer Alex Moulton, a collaboration which had begun with an experimental rubber-sprung Minor. Moulton initially equipped the V8-powered Alvis with a form of rubber springing and latterly with a rubber/fluid system; ultimately interconnected front to rear,

Artist's impression of the Alvis V8 saloon, specially commissioned for 'Classic and Sportscar' magazine. Features included a rear-mounted two-speed gearbox with double overdrive, and – in the car's final form – Moulton rubber suspension with fluid interconnection. Only one was built.

4

Before starting work on the Mini the Issigonis team worked on XC9001 (right), a rear-drive 1½ litre, and XC9002 (left), a planned front-wheel-drive Minor replacement which ultimately developed into the BMC 1100 model.

this was a prototype of the Hydrolastic system used in the future on the Mini and other BMC cars. Secondly, the Alvis period introduced Issigonis to John Sheppard and Chris Kingham, Alvis engineers who were to join him at BMC and be key members of the team behind the Mini.

On his return to BMC, as the combine's Chief Engineer, Issigonis led what would today be called a 'think tank' – a small group exploring future product concepts. The first prototype to emerge was a rear-wheel-drive 1½ litre saloon coded XC9001. Equipped with a development of the Alvis V8's Moulton fluid-and-rubber suspension, it had simple four-light styling which presaged that of the Mini. After this came a smaller car with similar looks, intended to be a replacement for the Minor. This time with front-wheel drive, it was called XC9002. Both projects were shelved to make way for the Mini, but they constituted key stages in the evolution of Issigonis's thoughts on automotive design.

Issigonis was an idiosyncratic and demanding taskmaster, communicating firmly held ideas in an uncompromising way. 'He knew where he wanted to go, he knew what he wanted, and that took months and months out of a programme, because there was no debate,' one senior engineer remembers.

A favourite way of explaining his requirements was through the detailed sketches for which he became famous and which were made on anything from a concrete floor to a restaurant tablecloth.

'He was a natural,' former BMC Chief Engineer Charles Griffin told the author. 'He hadn't got too much time for the mathematics, for the calculations. But he had that amazing eye, and he recognised that engineering followed natural laws. He was able to visualise things and put them down on paper in proportion, so that if a stress engineer picked up something he'd done, he'd find it uniformly correct, within small margins. In that respect he was pretty unique.'

Such a man was so invigorating to work for that his foibles were accepted. 'To be with him was absolutely inspirational. Everything he thought of was a challenge,' remembers John Sheppard.

The very first mock-up, in July 1957. At this stage the body lacked a bootlid and was 2 inches (51 mm) narrower than on the final production car. Coded XC9003, it is otherwise almost exactly as the Mini – a testament to the consistency of Issigonis's vision of the car.

DESIGN AND DEVELOPMENT

The team assembled around Issigonis in 1956-7 had a generally uninspiring mix of small cars to contemplate. The cheapest were the so-called 'bubble cars', of which the best-designed and longest-lived were the BMW-built Isetta, the Heinkel, and the tandem-seat Messerschmitt. Minimal runabouts with motorcycle-type engines, such vehicles enjoyed a brief vogue at the time of the Suez Crisis, and it was this popularity which prompted the BMC chief, Leonard Lord, to ask Issigonis to design something better.

Amongst the smaller 'proper' cars, the predominant layout on the continent was with the engine at the rear, the only exception being the front-wheel-drive Citroën 2CV – a design no less inspired than the Mini was to be.

Cheapness and lower engine noise were advantages of the rear-engine format, but compromised roadholding and handling were generally an unfortunate by-product. For Issigonis, such a trade-off was unacceptable, even without taking into account questions of space utilisation: good primary safety through high standards of chassis behaviour was always fundamental to his thinking.

In Britain there was nothing as daring as a rear-engined car – Rootes was to be the first and last to use such a layout, with the 1963 Hillman Imp. The prevailing wisdom, therefore, was to retain a conventional front-engine/rear-drive configuration, and the most compact example of this arrangement was BMC's own Austin A30/A35, at 11 feet 4³/₈ inches (3.46 metres) long.

In March 1957 Issigonis was instructed to begin work on a small car to drive the bubble cars from the roads. The only stipulation from Lord was that it should use a power unit derived from an engine already in production – in other words the A-series unit found in the Minor and the A35. For a while Issigonis experimented with a two-cylinder version of this engine, but it proved too rough and gutless; nonetheless, the 'twin' remained under consideration as an alternative power unit until at least mid 1958.

Issigonis had a clear and determined vision of what he wanted. Front-wheel drive with a transverse engine was a vital element: it would allow better use of space, improve traction and stability, and save weight. But this was only the start. Issigonis had a target length of only 10 feet (3.05 metres) for the car, yet he wanted it to be a full four-seater with adequate stowage space, rather than a cramped 2+2 such as the similarly sized Fiat 500. Such an aim could be achieved only by a design in which every element was interlinked, to produce a functional whole.

The first problem to be solved was how to mount an in-line four-cylinder engine transversely, yet in a small car still have room for the transmission. The answer was a bold one: to put the gearbox and final drive in the sump, sharing the same oil as the engine. The result, with the radiator side-mounted, was a power pack taking up only 18 inches (457 mm), leaving the rest of the car free for passengers and luggage.

To maximise this space, and to preserve correct proportions in a small car, Issigonis then stipulated 10 inch wheels – at a time when 13 inch wheels were the norm. Smaller wheels meant less wheelarch intrusion, and thus more internal space, and so Dunlop had to create suitable tyres for a relatively powerful four-seater saloon running on such small rims.

The suspension was as clever as one would expect, but it was not as originally intended. Alex Moulton had set up Moulton Developments with BMC and Dunlop in 1956, and he worked intensively on the perfection of his fluid-and-rubber suspension, later to become Hydrolastic, with a view to the Mini using it. Alas, attempts to miniaturise the system to fit the Mini proved a failure, and Moulton fell back on an evolution of the rubber spring unit first used on the Issigonis Alvis V8 saloon.

The resultant rubber-cone springs had three significant virtues: they were compact, they were light, and they offered the variable-rate characteristics desirable in a small and light car where the differing loads carried would vary so significantly as a proportion of the overall weight of the vehicle.

At the front – steered by rack and pinion – the suspension used single unequal-length arms acting on vertical rubber springs; at the rear there was an independent arrangement using trailing arms

The Mini rear subframe displays trailing arms and Moulton rubber 'cone' springs. Upright telescopic units provide the damping on these 'dry' Minis; on Hydrolastic cars the damping function is looked after by the water element of the fluid and rubber system.

7

A cutaway Mini demonstrates the car's extraordinary space efficiency. Note the early straight non-remote gear-lever, the baskets under the rear seats, and the pronounced curvature to the roof to allow extra headroom.

The Morris Mini-Minor, showing how the bootlid can form a luggage platform. The hinged rear number-plate was deleted after a few years, however, rendering such use illegal. The model is a De Luxe, identifiable by its opening rear windows, and would normally have rim embellishers as standard.

and horizontally disposed spring units. A beam rear axle had been considered, but intrusion into the boot ruled it out.

Getting the power to the wheels was another challenge. Conventional Cardan or Hooke joints would have a limited life, and the various existing types of constant-velocity joints were deemed unsatisfactory. In the end the Rzeppa joint, which at that time was being produced for submarine control gear, was adopted for the outer driveshaft coupling. The inner joints were initially of orthodox Hooke type, but after problems with drivetrain harshness these were replaced by rubber-insulated universals devised by Moulton.

The structure of the Mini was extremely simple and was conceived to be virtually self-jigging on the assembly line, owing to its external seams and – in its original form – its one-piece sides. At first the monocoque shell of the prototypes used a straightforward sheet-metal box to hold the engine and transmission, this structure being part welded and part bolted to the body. Substantial suspension loadings resulted in cracks appearing, so it was decided to change over to a separate subframe at the front and another at the rear, where similar problems had been encountered.

Another fundamental change was to turn the engine and transmission through 180 degrees. This was intended to combat carburettor icing experienced during winter testing, and it placed the carburettor behind the engine and thus the ignition system at the front, resulting in the notorious problem of water in the electrics suffered by early Minis in bad weather conditions.

More beneficial side effects were better cooling from the fan (allowing a 20 per cent reduction in radiator size), an easier route for the exhaust, and better synchromesh through the elimination of the large and heavy reduction gear used to transmit power from the engine to the gearbox. Unfortunately, though, the new east-west arrangement brought with it the addition of an intermediate reduction gear, and this idler gear not only added to noise but also caused a slight power loss.

Other changes during development included discarding a French-style push-pull dashboard gearchange because it transmitted too much noise to the passenger compartment, and widening the body by 2 inches (51 mm) for reasons of space utilisation and aesthetics. The risk of the brakes locking and provoking a skid was also tackled, by moving the battery from under the bonnet to the boot, and by fitting a pressure-balancing valve.

The increase in body width and the addition of the idler gear both helped lower the initial maximum speed of 92 mph (148 km/h), which was judged excessive, but it was nonetheless decided to reduce the engine's capacity from 948 cc to a more

The Austin Seven, again in De Luxe form. The crinkly grille was an Austin feature; apart from this, and different badging, Austin and Morris versions were identical. The Seven was renamed the Austin Mini in 1962.

modest 848 cc – at which size the production Mini developed 34 bhp net.

The body was intended to be purely functional – 'We're not selling a style, we're selling a tool that does a job, that gets people from A to B safely and cheaply,' Issigonis is remembered by John Sheppard as saying. But out of this functionalism came a shape of such rightness that Italian stylist Pininfarina pronounced it incapable of improvement.

Much of the cleverness was inside the car, beginning with the spacious and uncluttered shelf facing the driver and passenger and ending with the cubby holes under the rear seat, for which Issigonis devised little wicker baskets. Typical Issigonis touches were the large pockets in the doors and the rear quarters, and the refusal to bow to convention if to

do so meant to lose space. Consequently there were sliding front windows, to allow single-skin doors and thus more elbow room, and the steering column and the seats were more upright than normal, to give more vertical seating that took up less space. Finally, the boot revived pre-war practice by having a lid which could be let down to form a luggage platform.

Remarkably, such design innovation was achieved in a very short time: when the Mini was announced in the summer of 1959 it was after a gestation period of little more than two years. The total support of Lord was a key factor, in that he himself ensured that all BMC's resources were put at the Mini team's disposal, but ultimately it was the drive and vision of Alec Issigonis which saw the project through in a record time.

Morris Mini-Minor Traveller, with the painted Morris grille current on base and De Luxe models until October 1961; after then, the grille was chromed. The wood trim was purely ornamental, and from October 1962 a cheaper version was available without such adornment. All estates were to the De Luxe or the later Super De Luxe specification, and all had van-type twin rear doors.

THE RANGE EXPANDS

The result of all these endeavours was launched in August 1959 as the Austin Seven (spelt 'Se7en' by BMC) and the Morris Mini-Minor. The models were respectively advertised as 'A new breed of small car' and as 'Wizardry on wheels', the separate advertising campaigns emphasising the spurious differentiation of the two marques felt necessary at the time to appease the one-time rival dealer networks for Austin and Morris vehicles.

The received wisdom has always been that the car was slow to gain acceptance. In fact, in 1960, the Mini's first full year of production, a total of 116,677 were made, at both the Morris plant in Cowley and Austin's Longbridge factory. This was substantially more than the output of

75,345 Austin A35s achieved in 1958, the last full year of A35 saloon manufacture. In 1961, though, Mini sales jumped 34 per cent and in 1962 a hefty 47 per cent, so they did accelerate rapidly rather than progressively.

Unfortunately, early buyers were victims of various teething troubles from which the new car suffered. The best-known of these was the 'floating carpets' fiasco, when water mysteriously found its way into the car through the floor. It was eventually discovered that this was because the sill section had been designed the wrong way, and water was getting past the spot-welds. The prototypes were seam-welded and were tested during the dry summer of 1959, and so the problem escaped detection. Injecting the sills with foam effected a cure until the sills could be redesigned with the open join facing the other way.

Such faults were progressively eliminated, along with lesser ones, and what had begun as a two-model range of a saloon and a De Luxe saloon soon began to expand. The first variant, launched in May 1960, was a van, 10 inches (254 mm) longer and built on a wheelbase extended by 3 inches (76 mm); a pick-up followed in January 1961.

From the van was developed an estate car, introduced in September 1960 as the Morris Mini-Minor Traveller and the Austin Seven Countryman. With a flat floor measuring 12 square feet (1.1 square metres) with the rear seat folded, the estate was a superb load-carrier and offered up to 16 cubic feet (453 litres) of luggage space with the rear seat in use, against less than 6 cubic feet (170 litres) on the saloon.

In September 1961 came the Mini Super and the first Cooper. The Super was mechanically unchanged from the De Luxe but had improved seats, trim and carpets, an oval instrument nacelle incorporating water-temperature and oil-pressure gauges, better sound insulation, and lever-type interior door handles in place of pull-cables.

The Cooper was to the same trim and coachwork specification but had a long-stroke 997 cc engine with twin carburettors, tuned to deliver 55 bhp. There was also a close-ratio gearbox with a stubby remote change, and miniature 7 inch (178 mm) front disc brakes which almost doubled the braking area.

Devised by the racing-car constructor John Cooper, to whom royalties of £2 per car were paid, the Mini-Cooper was intended to be produced as a run of only one thousand cars, at a rate of 25 per week. But the car was so popular that in this first 997 cc form it ended up being turned out at the level of 750 examples each week. In November 1963 the Cooper received a revised engine of 998 cc, characterised by a bigger bore and a shorter stroke. Still delivering 55 bhp, it was smoother and much more torquey.

The Wolseley Hornet and Riley Elf were introduced a month later, in October 1961, carrying on the practice of 'badge engineering' through which BMC kept alive these two up-market marques, both of which had been purchased by Nuffield in the inter-war years. The Hornet and Elf were cleverly contrived pocket-sized luxury saloons, the Mini shape disguised by a projecting boot and by a Wolseley or Riley radiator grille lifting with the bonnet. The extra 2½ cubic feet (71 litres) of boot space was a bonus, but the additional weight – 1.2 cwt (61 kg) on the Hornet and 1.5 cwt (76 kg) on the Elf – dulled performance and prompted fit-

Cover illustration from a van and pick-up brochure. Shorter, lighter and with an 8 inch (203 mm) lower loading height than the preceding A35 van, the Mini van nonetheless had more load space. Unique to the commercials were the integral pressed-steel grille and the stowage of the spare wheel and battery behind the seats.

Mini-Minor Traveller without the timber. This 1965 example has a one-piece glass-fibre rear door, a popular 1960s after-market modification a one-piece tailgate was also found on some Portuguese-built Mini estates. This car's wheels are early Cosmic items.

Super interior – probably on a pre-production car. The oval three-dial instrument nacelle was shared with the Cooper and Cooper S and remained in use until 1980. Note the cranked gear-lever and the early type of door-pocket kick-plate: this soon gave way to a squared-off metal item.

Wolseley Hornet Mark I: the Hornet and Elf were clearly aimed at lady motorists, as this BMC publicity photograph makes clear. Pre-production Hornets featured a unique square instrument binnacle, centrally placed, but on production cars a veneer-trimmed version of the oval Super De Luxe binnacle was used.

How luxurious can an Austin Seven get?

Left: *Austin Super Seven, recognisable by the vertical bars on the grille, and the tubular overrider extensions; duotone colour schemes also featured. In October 1962 the De Luxe and the Super were amalgamated into a new Super De Luxe model, lacking such Super features as the vertically barred grille and the duotone paint.*

Right: *The Riley Elf interior: smartly appointed, it has a full-width wood-veneer dashboard. Seats on both Elf and Hornet are part-trimmed in leather.*

Mechanically identical to the Hornet, the Riley Elf differed only in its frontal treatment and its dashboard. A total of 30,912 Elves and 28,455 Hornets were built – a respectable score, but rather below the 99,281 Coopers (excluding the 'S') produced in the same 1961-9 period.

The second preproduction version of the Moke: the wheelbase is shorter, the ground clearance is better, and there are now side panniers in place of the previously open sides. This photograph dates from 1960, two years before the car in this form was shown at the Amsterdam motor show in a bid to attract military buyers.

14

ment of a 998 cc engine in 1963.

With 38 bhp instead of 34 bhp, and improved torque, these Mark II cars were much better; superior still were the Mark IIIs of 1966-9, which had wind-up windows (still with door pockets), face-level vents, and the Cooper's remote gearchange. Both models, however, were displaced in October 1969 by the arrival of the Mini Clubman.

The Coopers were more of a bread-winner, especially when the 1071 cc Cooper S arrived in March 1963. With a reduced stroke but a bigger bore, a new block had to be cast. Power output was 70 bhp, and maximum torque 62 lb ft (84 Nm) at a high 4500 rpm, but the important point was that the engine had been considerably strengthened to cope with further tuning. Naturally, the clutch and gearbox were also uprated, while the front discs were larger in diameter and thicker, with harder pads and the addition of a servo. Further helping braking – as well as roadholding – were offset vented wheels.

The 1071 cc Cooper S continued until August 1964. In March of that year two new Cooper S models were introduced: the 970 and the 1275. The more important was the 1275 cc version, the engine of which had a taller block to accommodate its longer stroke. The definitive Cooper S, the 1275 produced 76 bhp and delivered a maximum torque of 79 lb ft (107 Nm) at 3000 rpm, figures which translated into a car which was as flexible and untemperamental as it was high-performing.

The 970, in contrast, was smoother and higher-revving, with a performance not notably below that of the 1275, but with rather inferior torque delivery – 55 lb ft (75 Nm) at 3500 rpm. But that was not important because the 970 was a homologation special pure and simple, available only to order. Production ceased in January 1965 after only 972 had been built.

In contrast, the 1275 cc Cooper S survived until July 1971, taking on first Mark II and later Mark III guise; a total of 40,652 were manufactured.

The last Mini variant to appear in the BMC era was the Mini-Moke. Designed as a pack-flat motorised buckboard for the armed forces, the first prototypes were made in 1959. But the Army rejected the Moke on account of its limited ground clearance.

BMC tried again, with a more Jeep-like variant having a shorter wheelbase, increased ground clearance and the addition of a sump guard. There were still no takers. Management vetoed the fitting of bigger wheels 'for political reasons' – presumably they thought people would conclude that there was something wrong with the Mini's 10 inch wheels if they were abandoned for the Moke – and so Issigonis devised a more radical solution to the Moke's lack of off-road abilities.

This was to give it four-wheel drive by the simple expedient of installing a second engine and transmission, at the rear of the car. A 'Twini-Moke' went to the US Army for tests but again no orders were forthcoming, and so in 1964 the Moke entered production as a purely civilian vehicle.

'Twini-Moke': plenty of power and traction, but the two Mini gearchanges crudely linked together make changing gear a struggle. With the exception of the additional engine, necessitating a high rear deck and a shorter hood, it is virtually as production Mokes of 1964-8. Two 'Twini-Mini' saloons were also constructed but proved as troublesome as they were demanding.

The Kent firm Crayford offered a convertible version of the Mini in the 1960s and early 1970s. Initially, as in this 1963 photograph, the rear side windows were replaced by removable sidescreens; later cars, however, retained the original windows. The best-known Crayford Mini conversions were the 57 Wolseley Hornet convertibles made for Heinz in 1966, as competition prizes. The bonnet-mounted lamp nacelle is a period accessory.

Despite a certain Carnaby Street fashionableness, it was a failure – perhaps in part because the market for frivolous leisure cars was less developed than it is today. The Moke was spartan in the extreme, with poor weather protection, and owing to an unexpected liability for Purchase Tax it ended up, when fully equipped, as substantially more expensive than a Mini pick-up and not much cheaper than a basic Mini saloon. Only 14,518 were made before production moved to Australia in 1968. A bare 10 per cent of British-made Mokes were sold in the United Kingdom, which shows how ill-judged a project it was in commercial terms.

Manufacture continued in Australia until 1982, with ground clearance increased by the fitment of 13 inch wheels. In 1982 production moved to Portugal, and during the latter part of the decade a small but committed team at what became Austin-Rover Portugal considerably improved the car and boosted its sales. In 1990 the project was sold to an Italian company, which for a short while continued Moke production in Portugal.

Minisprint demonstrates its chopped lowline body. Current in the 1965-7 period, the conversion featured not only a lowered roof but also a slice taken out of the below-waist metalwork. The cars also lost their side body seams and, in some instances, their roof seam; additionally, some had rectangular headlamps.

Bizarre Minnow Mini GT of c.1966. Based on the pick-up, it has an add-on estate-type rear and a Minnow-Fish carburettor.

Late-model Innocenti Mini-Cooper 1300: fitment of quarter lights and use of different grille, headlamp rims and front indicators are features. Inside, more lavish trim includes a totally fresh dash design. This Italian Cooper S was current until the end of 1974.

FOREIGN VARIANTS, BRITISH EXPERIMENTATION, AND MODEL DEVELOPMENT

Over the years the Mini was assembled in many countries around the world, and some of these produced their own distinctive variants of the car.

The Italian firm Innocenti, for example, produced Minis equipped with Mark II grilles and Mark I rear lights, and when it changed over to wind-up windows it used a configuration incorporating quarter lights. In Australia, meanwhile, one could buy a long-nosed 'Clubman GT' with a Cooper S power unit and with wind-up windows and quarter lights set in pre-1970 doors with exposed hinges. In South Africa a Riley Elf shell fitted with a standard Mini front was offered.

These foreign specials were merely mild local adaptations of the familiar Mini. More radical were various transformations with which BMC itself experimented.

For instance, in 1960 BMC produced a long-wheelbase four-door Mini. Such a variant had been contemplated by Issigonis as early as 1957, presumably with an eye to a replacement for the four-door Austin A35, and the car as it emerged had a surprising elegance.

More tantalising were the various sports and GT cars devised around Mini running gear – despite Alec Issigonis making clear his objections to such space-wasting and unutilitarian designs. For example, there was a proposal by MG for a new Mini-based Midget. A prototype (ADO 34) was built, on a Mini van chassis, but it was not very elegant. There was also a scheme at Longbridge for a Mini-based MG coupé, at one stage on 13 inch wheels.

Rather better was another ADO 34 interpretation with styling by Pininfarina; nothing came of this, nor of a coupé version (ADO 35) which was also built. As late as 1970 the idea still had currency, however, and the Italian stylist Michelotti was commissioned to build a Targa-top coupé (ADO 70) on 1275 GT underpinnings.

Meanwhile, the Mini continued to evolve during the 1960s. This was in contrast to the 1970s, in the course of which it stagnated as the parent firm – the British Leyland Motor Corporation from 1968, British Leyland Ltd from 1975, and BL Ltd from 1978 – fought for survival.

The most significant modification came in September 1964, when the Mini received Hydrolastic suspension, though the estate cars and commercial vehicles retained the rubber cone set-up. Hydrolastic gave a softer but less well-

Another foreign special. This 1973 South African Mini GTS looks much like a 1275 GT but has silver-detailed Rostyle wheels, wheelarch spats and a twin-carb 1275 cc engine.

Long-wheelbase Mini prototype from 1960. Could it have been at least as successful as the Elf/Hornet, especially in those export markets where a four-door saloon was more appreciated than a two-door?

An MG version of the Mini Cooper S was mooted in 1963 and would have cost £18 more than the S. As well as the MG grille and Wolseley Hornet side grilles, the MG Mini would have had different seats and trim, a different dashboard (perhaps that of the Elf) and a wood-rim steering wheel.

The mock-up of a Mini-based MG coupé, dating probably from c.1960. This tantalising photograph was found by the author in the Rover Group's Longbridge archives.

18

Pininfarina's elegant little ADO 34 proposal for a Mini-based Sprite/ Midget replacement was built as an MG, but this 1966 Longbridge photograph shows a mock-up of a suggested Austin-Healey format, with a different grille. A coupé – ADO 35 – was also mooted.

controlled ride, and enthusiasts preferred the harsher original suspension; a possible remedy was to fit uprated Hydrolastic units from the BMC Competitions Department.

Then, in 1965, the Mini became available with a four-speed automatic transmission. To devise an automatic box for in-sump installation – and a four-speed one, moreover – was a major technical achievement. Alas, over the years relatively few people seem to have been impressed, with a 1977 survey showing that only one in twenty Mini buyers were choosing the automatic.

In 1967 the Mini received its first facelift. The new Mark II was given a 1 inch (25 mm) wider rear window, revised rear light clusters and a new grille, along with a smaller turning circle and brakes that were lighter to operate. On the Super De Luxe there were also better seats, a remote-control gearchange, and the 998 cc engine as standard, with a higher-geared final drive – although the 848 cc unit could still be specified. Additionally, from September 1968 bottom gear received synchromesh.

At the 1969 Motor Show there came what was advertised as 'The Big Happen-

ing'. This was the launch of the Mini Clubman, which in retrospect can be seen as rather a non-event. The new Mini – to be sold under that name alone and not as an Austin or a Morris – had a restyled and longer bonnet. It also had space-stealing wind-up front windows (as on the Mark III Elf/Hornet, but sacrificing the door pockets of those cars), face-level vents (again as the Mark III Elf/Hornet), improved seats, and a new dashboard with hard-to-read and less generous instrumentation. The Mini estates were replaced by a rubber-suspended Clubman estate with rust-inducing imitation-wood trim (eventually deleted), and the Cooper gave way to a new 1275 GT, with a single-carb 59 bhp engine.

A month later the short-nose Mini saloons received the Clubman's wind-up windows and its protruding rear number-plate lamp – and similarly lost their Austin or Morris identity to become plain Minis. Unofficially known as the 'Mark III', the revised cars were an 850 to standard specification (with – until the end of 1972 – the direct 'magic wand' gearchange), and a 1000 to Super De Luxe trim. Both had rubber-cone suspension, whereas the Clubman saloons and the

Charming Mini beach car, photographed in 1961. Although never a production model, BMC built quite a few of these, in various forms; this one has an Elf/Hornet rear and an odd frontal treatment.

One-piece glass-fibre bonnets were a popular 'boy-racer' modification in the 1960s and early 1970s. Rather different is this Scorpion front from 1967, fitting over the standard front wings and using an inverted Morris Mini grille. The wheels are JAP alloys, and the glass roof is an unusual fitting.

The Mini's subframe form of construction lent itself well to being a basis for kit cars. First in the field was Marcos, in 1966, with its glass-fibre Mini-Marcos shell. This spawned the Midas and is still in production in improved form.

An Austin Mini Super De Luxe Mark II displays its new bevelled grille; the squared-off tail lights also introduced with the Mark II are just visible. The unusual Status spats are a short-lived early 1970s accessory, as are the Dunlop alloy wheels; the front indicators are not of standard pattern.

1275GT retained Hydrolastic. This distinction lasted until June 1971, when Hydrolastic for the Mini was abandoned, primarily on grounds of cost.

There was little further change to the Mini during the 1970s. Changes other than cosmetic tinkering were primarily an im-proved and rod-actuated gearchange in 1973, 12 inch wheels on the 1275 GT in 1974, and a 1098 cc engine on all Clubmans except automatics in 1975. Additionally in 1979 the 850 became available in two variants: a base City model and a Super De Luxe version.

Ralph Broad, renowned for tuning Minis, devised this coupé, which had a glass-fibre superstructure incorporating a more steeply raked screen and a DB6-like rear. Various specifications were offered, the most elaborate having a tweaked Broadspeed 1275 cc engine and a revised interior with a full-width dashboard. A total of 28 were built, many going to Spain.

During all this time Mini sales were generally buoyant. After a series of yearly rises, production dipped in 1965 and 1966, but thereafter it rose by respectable amounts each year until 1971. From then on, ever stronger competition from more modern 'Supermini' hatchbacks – and a growing distrust of British Leyland – caused production, solely at Longbridge from 1969, to fall a little each year: from a peak of 318,475 in 1971 output had by 1978 tumbled by more than a third, to 196,502 vehicles. The following year there was a slide to 165,502. In 1981, the first full year of Metro manufacture, output dropped to 69,986.

To sell 200,000 to 300,000 of any model per year is creditable, even today, but in the Mini's case there has always been one important question: was the car making money for its manufacturer?

To this there is no clear answer, although BMC did itself little good by pricing the car below the antiquated A35 it replaced. Early on, Ford stripped and costed a Mini and concluded that there was a £30 loss on each car; higher-priced later variants, however, may have been

Clubman estate – the real but ornamental wood of previous Mini estates gave way to even more contrived dummy-wood strakes, continued around the rear doors. Wind-up windows brought with them concealed door hinges, and the extended bonnet made servicing marginally more easy.

The 1275 GT was billed as a Cooper successor. With 59 bhp it was more potent than the 998 cc Cooper, but no match for the Cooper S. Later cars had higher gearing, less power and 12 inch wheels, latterly of Denovo 'runflat' type.

All that was left in 1981: the former Clubman estate, rebadged 1000HL, has lost its vertical grille divider and displays the striping introduced in 1977, while the saloons have matt black grilles with short-lived Austin-Morris emblems.

The Clubman interior from 1969 shows better-profiled seats, air vents, a new steering wheel and a twin-dial instrument binnacle in front of the driver. Unfortunately the instrumentation no longer included an oil-pressure gauge, and the dials were difficult to read.

more viable. By 1968 it was calculated that the Mini was bringing in a profit – £15 or £35, depending on source. Ten years later, BL could say that the Mini was making a modest profit at home but reporting a loss in export markets. After another decade, prices had been raised to such a degree that the Rover Group boss Sir Graham Day could pronounce the Mini 'a nice little earner'.

In conclusion it can be said that at best the Mini always provided modest profits for its manufacturer, and that the situation can only have improved with more efficient manning practices and more modern production techniques.

Final thoughts for a Mini-based coupé: coded ADO 70, this was an exercise commissioned from Michelotti in 1970. It was seen as a possible replacement for the Midget and Sprite. The roof is a two-part removable Targa design.

Customised Minis had begun with Harold Radford's charming upper-crust conversions of the 1960s; by the following decade they had degenerated into such exercises as this 'Mini Margrave', offered by Wood and Pickett.

The BMC Competitions Department at Abingdon, in 1966, with cars under preparation for that year's Monte Carlo Rally. In the foreground is a Cooper S subframe, with a Hydrolastic displacer clearly visible; the perforated wheels are an S trademark.

THE MINI IN COMPETITION

In its original 848 cc form, the Mini was too low-powered to be successful in international rallying, and the best results achieved by BMC's works entries were tenth overall on the 1960 Tulip Rally and class wins in the same year's Geneva and Alpine rallies and in the 1961 Tulip. The Mini's early participation in the Monte Carlo Rally was hardly auspicious, either: a highest placing of 23rd in 1960 and the retirement of all three works cars the following year.

But at the end of 1961 the 997 cc Mini-Cooper gave BMC the power – and the front disc brakes – it needed: with bigger carburettors and only modest tuning the Cooper's 55 bhp output rose to 70 bhp, giving the Mini a power to weight ratio to match its roadholding and handling. At the same time Stuart Turner, a respected rally navigator, took over the BMC Competitions Department at Abingdon and brought a new professionalism to the team.

In May 1962 the Mini secured its first international rally victory, when Pat Moss and Ann Wisdom won the Tulip Rally. Outright wins in the Baden-Baden and Geneva rallies followed.

This progress was consolidated in 1963, when Rauno Aaltonen came in third overall in the Monte Carlo Rally, with Paddy Hopkirk finishing sixth. The real breakthrough, though, came with the introduction in March 1963 of the 1071 cc Mini-Cooper S. No sooner was it in production than Aaltonen had taken it to victory in the Alpine Rally and Hopkirk to a third overall – and first on handicap – in the Tour de France. With a fourth place in the RAC Rally at the end of the year, it was clear that the Mini was now a force with which to be reckoned – helped by the slickly run Competitions Department and a number of talented Scandinavian drivers to complement the British team members.

This message was confirmed in 1964, with the Mini's first victory in the Monte Carlo Rally, after an epic drive by Hopkirk. Nor was that all: with Timo Makinen coming in fourth and Rauno

*Rauno
Aaltonen and
Tony Ambrose
in full flight on
the 1966
Monte Carlo
Rally.*

Aaltonen seventh, the Mini team won the Manufacturer's Prize for BMC.

In March 1964 the 1275 S arrived. Initially, though, the bigger-engined Cooper suffered from reliability problems, and after a win in the Tulip Rally the latter part of the season was patchy for the Abingdon team, culminating in a disastrous RAC Rally in which all four works Minis retired.

Such setbacks were soon forgotten, however, owing to the phenomenal successes of 1965, beginning with a second victory in the Monte Carlo Rally; this time it was Makinen's turn, and in atrocious conditions he was the only driver to finish the rally without lateness penalties. During the year the BMC team achieved eight European rally victories and in the Alpine Rally the four Mini crews won no fewer than 27 cups, the biggest ever tally by any works team. At the end of 1965 Rauno Aaltonen, having scored five of BMC's eight victories, was declared European Rally Champion.

In 1966 it was much the same story of Mini dominance, with victory in eight international rallies. It was also the year of the infamous Monte Carlo Rally in which the Minis came in first, second and third, but were disqualified by the French organisers on a trumped-up lighting technicality.

This generated much sympathetic publicity for the British team and made the Mini's victory in the 1967 Monte Carlo Rally all the sweeter. But 1967 was to be the Mini's last year as a dominant force in rallying.

Budget cuts at the ailing BMC were only part of the reason. Porsche were now strong contenders in rallying and had much more power at their disposal, and in addition bigger and more specialist machinery from Lancia and Alpine was beginning to make itself felt; then there was Ford, who in 1968 would begin fielding the new Escort, in twin-cam form.

To stay successful, BMC would have to squeeze more power from the Mini and evolve the rest of the mechanicals to match. Yet with the Mini's A-series engine having a capacity tied to around the 1.3 litre mark, and no alternative power unit in prospect, there was limited scope for going beyond the 130 bhp achieved with the fuel-injected 1293 cc Mini devised for the cancelled 1967 RAC Rally.

Still, despite such concerns, the 1967 season brought six outright wins and nine class victories. It was to be a different story in 1968, with a third, fourth and fifth in the Monte Carlo Rally being accompanied by a cluster of class wins in lesser rallies. The following year Mini rally participation petered out and the BMC works rally team was disbanded; in 1970 came the Mini's final bow in international rallying, when Paddy Hopkirk took an Abingdon-prepared 1275GT to second place in the Scottish Rally.

In racing, as with rallying, it took the arrival of the Cooper to bring success. Nevertheless, there were full grids of Minis by 1961 in BRSCC events, and Sir John Whitmore went on to win that year's BRSCC Touring Car Championship in his tweaked 848 cc Mini. Additionally, the 750 Motor Club had established two special Mini race series, the Mini Se7en and Mini Miglia championships.

With the coming of the Mini-Cooper,

A race at Brands Hatch in 1966. The front Cooper (presumably an S despite its lack of badging) is a Morris and so has coarser grille slatting than the Austin Mini-Cooper S behind. This distinction was not preserved in the Mark II cars.

BMC supported the Cooper Car Company to field a team of 997 cc Minis, and in 1962 John Love won the BRSCC British Saloon Car Championship.

From this stage on, the pace was stepped up, with several teams entering the fray and spectacular close-packed racing being the order of the day – not just between the rival Mini teams but between the Minis and far bigger and more powerful saloons such as Jaguars and Ford Galaxies. Here the spectators' hero was John Rhodes, whose determined tyre-smoking style was dramatic in the extreme.

A fresh twist came in 1969, when BMC's rally team was disbanded and an Abingdon-based BMC racing team created in opposition to the Cooper team. But it was Team Arden's Alec Poole, in a 1 litre Cooper S, who won that year's British Saloon Car Championship.

During the 1970s the Mini – often heavily modified – continued to be a mainstay of club racing, but in the upper echelons of saloon-car racing it was eclipsed by faster machinery. In compensation, there was the new sport of rallycross, devised in 1967 as a television entertainment, and which soon became a Mini fiefdom – leading in 1978 to the creation of a special low-cost Mini-only series called Minicross.

In the late 1970s, however, the Mini made a racing comeback, in the slightly modified 'Group $1^1/_2$' British Saloon Car Championship. The experienced Mini driver Richard Longman won the championship in 1978 and 1979.

Under-bonnet view of one of the 1965 Monte Carlo cars: a tight fit for everything, and a superb level of preparation. The production S engine had among its modifications a nitride-hardened and more robust steel crankshaft, toughened valves and improved oil circulation and thus could comfortably stand the extra tuning the rally cars were given.

The so-called 'barrel car' was intended to preserve the Mini's basic shape, but to gain more room by giving the sides a pronounced curvature. The front styling on this studio mock-up is similar to that of the BMC 1800.

REPLACING THE MINI

The Mini's creator, Alec Issigonis, was a forward-thinking engineer ever eager to advance automotive design. Had he been allowed complete freedom, the Mini – having spawned the bigger 1100/1300 and 1800 – would have been replaced with a new model by the beginning of the 1970s.

Always happiest with small cars, Issigonis created a new Mini in 1968 – drawing on work on a 'mini-Mini' already carried out for Innocenti. Within the same wheelbase as the Mini and an overall length 4 inches (102 mm) less, the astonishing '9X' hatchback actually had more interior room – a packaging coup never since equalled.

Part of the secret was an all-new engine. With an alloy head, separate alloy crankcase and alloy sump, the lightweight cogged-belt overhead-camshaft unit was made unusually narrow by putting the oil pump on the nose of the crankshaft and by fitting a flywheel alternator, motorcycle-style. It developed a strong 60 bhp per litre – an impressive figure even today. Furthermore, the engine was also tried in 1300 cc six-cylinder format, where it gave both superb smoothness and surprisingly good economy.

There was also a new gearbox of sim-

The Issigonis 9X was an extraordinary packaging achievement, largely because of its extremely compact engine. This power unit was also developed in six-cylinder form, in which guise it was experimentally installed in a Metro with apparently impressive results.

Innocenti's rebodied Mini had lines by Bertone; a front radiator featured. After Innocenti had been sold to De Tomaso the model continued and was ultimately fitted with a Daihatsu three-cylinder engine and conventional coil-spring suspension. Production ceased in 1992.

pler and less noisy design; suspension was by strut at the front and transverse torsion bars at the rear, giving a soft if less well-controlled ride.

With 42 per cent fewer components than the Mini, 9X would have been significantly cheaper to produce. The last car to be designed by Issigonis, it was arguably his greatest achievement after the Mini itself. Alas, the frail health of BMC led to the merger with Leyland, and a combination of internal politics and the pressing need to produce a new mid-range car put paid to this exciting project.

At around the same time BMC engi-

neers were working on another idea: to create more space in the existing Mini by rebodying it with more outwardly curving panels. The so-called 'barrel car' remained a styling exercise, however.

It was not until 1972 that British Leyland gave serious thought to replacing the Mini. By this time there was strong international competition from the Fiat 127, Renault 5 and Datsun Cherry – all bigger and more refined cars than the Mini.

Three possible designs were considered: one roughly the same size as the Mini, but with more luggage space and an optional hatchback; one the same size as the

This ugly Mini is a Leyland 'Experimental Safety Vehicle', one of a family shown in the early 1970s. The structure is substantially beefed up, there is a heavily padded and claustrophobic cabin, and the droop-snoot front with its low bumper is intended to scoop a hit pedestrian on to the bonnet rather than knock him or her flat.

On the way to the Metro countless styling approaches were tried. This 1975 proposal was one of several which tried to retain a feel of the original car in its lines. The 'Mini' badging indicates that at this stage ADO 88 was seen as a direct replacement for the Issigonis car.

Fiat and Renault; one more akin to the Fiat 128 and Simca 1100 in size, and with a three-box body. The logic of the last scheme is unclear, but such ponderings were soon discarded, and efforts focused on a car 11 feet 6 inches (3.5 metres) long – roughly 127 size. This was despite British Leyland's overseas sales arm wanting a smaller car preserving the fashionable compactness of the Mini.

Overseas markets, however, did have just such a Mini. This was the Bertone-styled Mini hatchback introduced in 1975 by Innocenti. As foreign rivals snatched ever more sales from the Mini, and with there being no sign of a modern replacement or an update of the existing design, critics lamented British Leyland's failure to produce – or even sell – the Innocenti in Britain.

The answer given was that although the snappy Italian hatchback was 3 inches (76 mm) longer and 3½ inches (89 mm) wider than the Mini, it offered no more room inside; it would also have been more costly to build. Given the five-year gap before a new Mini arrived, it is not unreasonable to ask whether British production of the Innocenti, at a profitable premium price, might not have proved an invaluable holding operation. Or would this have merely taken sales from the Mini, thereby reducing the original car's financial viability?

Meanwhile, design work on a genuine Mini replacement proceeded. Then came the collapse of British Leyland, and its subsequent nationalisation in 1975. Under new management, ADO 74, as it was tagged, gave way to ADO 88.

Intended to be smaller than ADO 74, yet with interior room unsurpassed in its class, this project, substantially revised and recoded LC8, emerged in October 1980 as the Austin Metro. Was this the end of the Mini?

Special editions flourished in the 1980s and 1990s. These two, 'Jet Black' and 'Red Hot', display the 12 inch wheels introduced on the Mini in 1984, and necessitating the use of plastic wheelarch spats. The bigger wheels brought with them the front disc brakes previously the preserve of the Coopers and the 1275 GT.

THE MINI'S TWILIGHT YEARS

In the run-up to the Metro launch it was assumed – if never quite believed – that after the new car's arrival the Mini would quietly fade away. This was not the plan, and BL stressed that the Mini would remain in production. Meanwhile, in June 1980 it was given a comprehensive and long overdue noise-suppression kit, and in August the City received the 1000 cc engine.

With the October 1980 fanfare launch of the Metro, the Clubman saloon and the 1275 GT were deleted and the Mini 1000 and Clubman estate were given improved equipment and renamed Mini HL; the former Clubman estate reverted to the 998 cc engine – albeit, as on all Minis from then on, the revised and more efficient A-plus unit.

In April 1982 the higher-geared economy-tune Metro HLE power pack was fitted to the Mini, and the models renamed City E and Mini HLE; two months later, in June 1982, the estate car was discontinued, although the related van and pick-up survived until December. In September the HLE was replaced by the slightly plusher Mayfair model.

After 1982 the Mini remained largely unchanged, with only two significant developments. The first came in October 1984, when the 12 inch wheels and disc front brakes first seen on the 1275 GT became standard equipment. The second modification, in spring 1992, was forced by emissions legislation and was a move to the 1275 cc engine, still carb-fed; this allowed the fitting of a catalyst and slightly increased power to 50 bhp.

During the 1980s and 1990s the lack of changes to the Mini was accompanied by a deluge of special edition models: in the period 1983–2000 there were over thirty such variants.

The cynics might abhor these as a cheap marketing gimmick, but according to Rover they increased Mini sales and were a 'promotional focal point' for the model. Over 25 per cent of 1992 Mini output was of special editions, so the exercise was clearly a worthwhile one.

Even more successful as a marketing initiative was the revival of the Mini-Cooper. Launched in July 1990 with a 61 bhp single-carb 1275 cc engine, it was fitted with single-point fuel-

Sold through the Austin Rover dealer network, the ERA Mini Turbo was launched in 1988 by engineering consultancy ERA. It used the MG Metro Turbo power unit, developing 94 bhp, and had modified suspension and brakes. The body kit was styled by Dennis Adams, responsible for the lines of Marcos cars.

After years of sitting on their hands, the makers of the Mini finally reinstated the 1275 cc engine in 1990 and re-created the Mini-Cooper. This is the introductory limited edition, with John Cooper's signature on the bonnet stripes.

injection in October 1991 – a move giving the car only a fraction more power, but more measurably improved torque.

The Cooper was introduced to attract more male buyers, and in the early 1990s it accounted for between 30 and 40 per cent of total Mini output. Despite the supposedly more masculine appeal of the Cooper, however, sales of the Mini remained predominantly to women – 77 per cent, at last count; furthermore, the average age of a Mini buyer was 45 years old. Indeed, 1997 Rover figures show that more people over 65 (16 per cent) were

In 1993 the Rover Group put on sale this cabriolet Mini, as a follow-on to a German-built soft-top that had received factory backing. With a luxury interior and a full body-kit, the Longbridge-assembled cabriolet cost £11,995 in 1993, against £6995 for an injected Cooper.

buying the Mini than people in the 17–24 year-old bracket, who accounted for only 13 per cent of sales. The Mini's appeal to the young was based, it would appear, on the purchase of second-hand examples.

Production of the Mini fell sharply after 1980. In 1981, the first year after the Metro was introduced, it dropped to 69,986, and by 1986 the figure had slumped to 33,740. The car was not being advertised, and it was discovered that many thought the Mini was no longer in production. Worse, management were planning to axe the car by the end of 1987.

It took the arrival in 1986 of a new chairman, Sir Graham Day, to reverse the decline by throwing his weight behind the continued manufacture of the car. After a further drop in production to 31,979 in 1988, output at Longbridge leapt to 40,998 a year later, and to 46,045 in 1990. A key factor was the cult 'retro' status of the Mini in Japan: by 1992 the Japanese were taking 26.9 per cent of Mini output, making Japan a bigger market for the Mini than the United Kingdom itself.

Unfortunately the early 1990s slump led to annual sales levelling out at approximately 20,000 units. Despite this, Rover Group, as BL was renamed in 1986, boldly proclaimed in 1993 that 'there is no level below which the Mini ceases to be viable'. That continued to be the case, but for dif-

ferent reasons, after BMW's 1994 acquisition of Rover and the decision to launch a new Mini: building the Mini 'brand' would be easier with the original still alive.

So, despite dwindling sales, the Mini – fuel-injected since 1994 – was substantially modified for 1997 so it would continue to meet safety and emissions requirements. All versions were given a 1275 cc multipoint-injected 63 bhp engine and received a front radiator to meet noise regulations; a driver's airbag was also fitted and the doors strengthened with anti-intrusion beams. Equipment levels were raised, the Sprite dropped, and a long list of 'retro' accessories introduced. Prices rose to £9000 – nearly £2000 more than a basic Rover 100 then cost. Unsurprisingly, this further move away from the Mini's original role as low-cost transport caused sales to fall even further, and in 1999 a mere 11,738 cars left the Longbridge works.

With BMW's disengagement from Rover in 2000, the German company took the new Mini with it, moving the production site from Longbridge to Cowley, and delaying the car sales début until summer 2001. In the interim, manufacture of the Issigonis original ended on 4th October 2000. Production in the last year amounted to a slender 7069 cars, bringing the grand total to 5,387,862 units over 41 years.

FURTHER READING

Baggott, John. *Mini – The Racing Story*. Crowood, 1999.
Bardsley, Gillian. *Issigonis – The Official Biography*. Icon, 2005.
Barker, Ronald, and Harding, Anthony (editors). *Automobile Design: Great Designers and Their Work*. David & Charles, 1970.
Booij, Jeroen. *Maximum Mini*. Veloce, 2009.
Browning, Peter. *The Works Minis*. Haynes, 1971; new editions 1979, 1996.
Chambers, Marcus, Turner, Stuart and Browning, Peter. *BMC Competitions Department Secrets*. Veloce, 2005.
Filby, Peter. *Amazing Mini*. Haynes, 1981; new edition 1987.
Golding, Rob. *Mini*. Osprey, 1979; regular new editions.
Hopkirk, Paddy. *The Paddy Hopkirk Story*. Haynes, 2005.
Hübner, Johannes. *The Big Mini Book*. Bay View Books, 1992.
Moylan, Bryan. *Anatomy of the Works Minis*. Veloce, 2001.
Nahum, Andrew. *Alec Issigonis*. The Design Council, 1988.
Parnell, John. *Original Mini-Cooper and Cooper S*. Bay View Books, 1993; new edition Motorbooks, 2002.
Pomeroy, Laurence. *The Mini Story*. Temple Press, 1964.
Pressnell, Jon. *Morris Minor – The Official Photo Album*. Haynes, 2008.
Pressnell, Jon. *Mini – The Definitive History*. Haynes, 2009.
Price, Bill. *The BMC Competitions Department*. Haynes, 1989; reprinted 1998.
Rees, Chris. *The Complete Mini*. Motor Racing Publications, 1994; new edition 2003.
Robson, Graham. *Metro – The Book of the Car*. Patrick Stephens, 1982.
Sharratt, Barney. *Men and Motors of 'The Austin'*. Haynes, 2000.
Turner, Stuart. *Twice Lucky – My life in Motorsport*. Haynes, 1999.
Wood, Jonathan. *Alec Issigonis: The Man who made the Mini*. Breedon, 2005.

In addition, Brooklands Books have published excellent compilation volumes of magazine articles on the Mini, Mini-Cooper and Mini-Moke.

PLACES TO VISIT AND CLUBS

PLACES TO VISIT
There are many museums in Britain which have large collections of cars, but the following are known to have Minis. Readers are advised to check opening times before travelling. An up-to-date list of all road-transport museums in the United Kingdom can be found on www.motormuseums.com

Heritage Motor Centre, Banbury Road, Gaydon, Warwickshire CV35 0BJ. Telephone: 01926 641188. Website: www.heritage-motor-centre.co.uk
Lakeland Motor Museum, Old Blue Mill, Backbarrow, Ulverston, Cumbria LA12 8TA. Telephone: 015395 58509/30400. Website: www.lakelandmotormuseum.co.uk
National Motor Museum, John Montagu Building, Beaulieu, Brockenhurst, Hampshire SO42 7ZN. Telephone: 01590 612345. Website: www.beaulieu.co.uk

CLUBS
British Mini Club: David Hollis, The Mini House, 18 Aldgate Drive, Amblecote, Brierley Hill, West Midlands DY5 3NT. Telephone: 01384 897779. Website: www.britishminiclub.co.uk
Mini-Cooper Register: Lesley Young, Spring Cottage, Small Hythe, Tenterden, Kent TN30 7NF. Telephone: 01580 763975. Website: www.minicooper.org
Mini-Marcos Owners' Club: Roger Garland, 28 Meadow Road, Claines, Worcester WR3 7PP. Telephone: 01905 458533.
Mini-Moke Club: Louisa Upton, 9 Chestnut Avenue, Wootton, Northants NN4 6LA. Telephone: 01604 674750. Website: www.mokeclub.org
National Mini Owners' Club: Chris Cheal, 15 Birchwood Road, Lichfield, Staffordshire WS14 9UN. Telephone: 01543 257956. Website: www.miniownerslub.co.uk

In addition to these national clubs there are sundry regional and more specialist groupings.